In *godhouse*, Ruth Ellen Kocher divines the multidimensional gods and monsters that live within us slipping between terror and beauty, beginnings and endings, what is found and what is lost, "nothing...and everything at once." Innovative in their paratactic shifts, pliable syntax, and surprising juxtapositions, these poems embrace the personal, mythical, historical, ecological, socio-political, and cosmological as lived, embodied experience. In its polyphony, the collection collapses imagined boundaries between beings—"(let's do the math): you are I are thou/exponentially"—yet never forgets that "clarity is not white" and that "anything can become a grenade." When Kocher declares, "I can hold a pen like a weapon / I can hold a key between two fingers / straight out like a spike / and call it how to walk home," she's on her way to the *godhouse*, and I'm walking right beside her. —Brenda Cárdenas, author of *Trace*

godhouse reveals the gorgeously pitched trajectory of Kocher's lyric powers and blazing intellect, where language beguilingly constellates and historizes and frees the body eternally into a vast monument. My admiration is boundless at how these poems transmit the hidden with elegance and brings to fore a complex tenderness I had not known I desired,"a viral expansion of light." —Major Jackson, author of *The Absurd Man*

Ruth Ellen Kocher's devastating collection of poems, *godhouse*, prefigures grief in its emergence from "blunder" and "nothing." Like Ralph Ellison's "Invisible Man," the speaker in Kocher's *godhouse* holds a knife in her teeth against a shadow world of hunter and hunted in which survival is necessarily mystical. Unnerved and unnerving these poems are a barbiturate gaze's disinhibition through the tattered dystopia of an American life. Heady, emotional, and meticulously crafted, *godhouse* leaves no room for delusion in its blade, pointed right at whomever might pose a threat. —Dawn Lundy Martin, author of *Good Stock Strange Blood* (Kingsley Tufts Poetry Award)

godhouse

Cover art by Michael Tella
cover art title: Queen of Ivory

Cover design by Laura Joakimson and Ruth Ellen Kocher
Interior design by Laura Joakimson
Cover typeface: Brother 1816
Interior typeface: Hightower and Brother 1816

Library of Congress Cataloging-in-Publication Data

Names: Kocher, Ruth Ellen, 1965- author.
Title: Godhouse / Ruth Ellen Kocher.
Description: Oakland, California : Omnidawn Publishing, 2023. | Summary:
"If the human experience is the equivalent of the universe looking back
at itself, godhouse takes that notion a few steps further by centering
cosmology in a raced and gendered body, in a union of god and soul that,
within our material world, easily vacillates between love and hate, joy
and despair. The body manifests as divine presence made mortal, as an
infinity singing the generative human arc of being-ness with an electric
resonance. In godhouse, the reader encounters the universe made personal
and celebratory, as an infinity that endures the complications of flesh
and the necessary resistance to our most ungodly and monstrous
expressions of personhood"-- Provided by publisher.

Identifiers: LCCN 2023019300 | ISBN 9781632431165 (trade paperback)
Subjects: LCGFT: Poetry.
Classification: LCC PS3561.O313 G63 2023 | DDC 811/.54--dc23/eng/20230427
LC record available at https://lccn.loc.gov/2023019300

Published by Omnidawn Publishing, Oakland, California
www.omnidawn.com
10 9 8 7 6 5 4 3 2 1
ISBN: 978-1-63243-116-5

godhouse

ruth ellen kocher

OMNIDAWN PUBLISHING
OAKLAND, CALIFORNIA
2023

table of contents

preface

By the time we get to the godwilling ballpark middle of our lives, or the middle of our writing lives, as this book of Ruth Ellen Kocher's, her eighth, maybe represents, a kind of midway contention, a kind of gathering up and re-assessing, which includes in some way also a re-telling or re-imagining of one's life, one's language, one's stories, one's histories, one's mythologies, I think we think, or maybe I should just speak for myself, I think I have thought, though I don't think I'm alone in this, that the ground might get stable, the footing sound, the sound found, and familiar: a bell the shape of which we know down to our blood and bones, and the song of which, and the ringing, and the dancing to which, and the mourning, and the dreaming, we get, or think we do anyway, all the way down. We get it down.

Indeed, one might contend this is the hope of such a work as *godhouse*, whose astonishing beauty is the evidence of years of labor, inquiry, practice, struggle, and, in a certain frame of mind, mastery; *godhouse* might be the evidence precisely of how one might nail into place not only one's meandrous and nearly unfathomable origins, but too the puzzle, or rather, the cosmos, into which those origins dropped you. The hope sometimes is to nail the cosmos we are into place. A poet, after all, in the old-timey (Greek etc.) sense of the word, is a maker. The pen or pencil a screwdriver, a hammer. And the raw material of one's life, one's observation, one's understanding, one's language, plus music, plus form, fixed into a craft in which to sail safely, and finally, on home.

Per the craft: I know of few poets whose vessels are as beautiful, as well-built, as Kocher's. It has been astonishing, and moving, to witness and study her work over these past, well, decades (full disclosure: Ruth is a bit of a big sister to me, and a big sister in poetry, since we met at Cave Canem in 2004; she has read my poems, she has pointed me this way and that, we read the Duino Elegies of

Rilke—who peeks through at least one of these poems—together on a sunny hill, or a glade, in St. Louis in 2005, we went the wrong day to Lorca's house in Seville and so peeked in the windows in 2006), which seems always to me turning toward something else. Or turning into something else. Or, as she writes in "Cosmogony", the opening poem in *godhouse*, "I begin with" and "I begin at" and "I begin in" and "I begin as," which I can't help but read as my beginning never ends (and my ending never begins). Which maybe is connected to why Kocher's poems in *godhouse* mostly refuse the sentence: they require a grammar that does not finish us, does not complete us or lock us up; they require a grammar in which we are perpetually becoming. Also per the craft: oh the language, the voicings: how many times reading this book I have put my hand to my heart, to my throat, reaching for my voice, for how beautifully she sings: "I was a lurch called girlhood until the cancer came"; or, "i am the arch / beneath your heart cramp / your deciduous reach // the splenetic / fabric of your spine / i am the night's / stampede"; or, "what prone light enters un-feathered now." If you, like me, are a gasper at a beautiful line, or an unfurling of them, you will gasp. You will be breathless. Hers is an elegant and annihilating diction. On and on like this, poem after poem, Kocher builds for us a craft that undoes its tether to the dock, or the shore; Kocher crafts a vessel that unmoors, and we with it.

Here's what I think I'm trying to say: Kocher's *godhouse* reminds me that as much as a poem is a making, and a poet a maker, poems too, maybe more to the point, are unmakings, and their poets unmakers. And the job—by which I mean the labor and the practice and the years and the books—is not mastery, nor is it getting it down. The job is getting down. By which I probably mean getting with. Listening, you know? As the musicians will tell us. As any relationship worth its salt, worth its honey, will tell us. Listening; you know. To be undone, unmoored, unmade into one another, that's what the craft's for. What the labor and the practice is for. To take us where our beginning never ends, and our ending never begins. –Ross Gay

i

cosmogony

i begin with ocean
floating in the free space of my ribs
somewhere between
ursa major and ursa minor
i begin in scorpio
a car ride into the city
before andromeda collided with the milky way another timeline ago
i begin as a cluster of muscadine grapes bursting bloody on their stems
i begin at the end
hungry
gorged on the ill-shaped stars which had
not yet begun
i begin beaten by my own hands
a comet galaxy
orbiting the parking lot of stumblin' inn friday nights waiting for a wrong turn
in the right car
i begin as a side bet
a detour into cosmos
via the elliptical path of my thumbprint
i begin as magellan's cloud hovering above
a cartwheel galaxy before magellan imagined himself
i begin as a call into
the deep-deep
as a black eye begging my way into medusa merger
i begin
as something found and then lost
as a clutch
meaning a small group
as in a small group of mothers huddled around a baby fever-charged
i begin with nothing
no history   no moons

i imagine nothing and
nothing begins

how i am born

three days before
my mother dies
she says
i'm glad i kept you

cephalogenesis

in november
a lie fertilizes an embryo

in december
panic begins

in january
her mother calls her *whore*

the northeastern sky is crisp
brutal

the trees are raked hands
everywhere

in a very fine suit
malcolm is gunned down

february
has no mercy

the bullet tunnels
a quantum path

through the badlands
behind time

march is bloody
selma will never heal

july becomes my body becoming

a terror

the skull of a century
splits in two

my mother tells me i am a god
i believe her

when i am born

my body stories in fits
squalls of *then what happened*
or *before she whispered*
or *the trees that year*
as though the narrative trail
from birth to whatever happens
might be more benediction than prologue
as if the remains of memory
circle and tide our mortal shores
i come to this life as a blunder
as the candor of spent sheets
one slow fertile morning
he was an asshole
but so handsome
at first i armor
my bliss
i undo the nothing
from which i come
i fling myself into telling
myself about myself
brawl upper air with
righteous happening

lapsarian

the first god was stolen from her home   or
her home was stolen from her

her home is being stolen now since
all time is the same

when i say *body*
i mean *monster*
when i say *time*
i mean *land*

i say *we*
instead of *cosmos*
as in
we embrace a fleshed affliction

when a god consumes a body
the body can only crave

forget *gods*
think
monsters
un-homed
we're the same

god of ways

in our contract as gods we agree first
to leave the everything we make to its own devices
meaning the fractal formed by an infinite system
bumping up against the impossibility of logical conclusion
backwards into space-time weaving coastlines
from the silt of our godly imaginations which likewise
fill a multidimensional nothing nothing nothing
nothing and everything at once which is also how love
comes accidentally into being not the human love
all love has now become but the interwork of godhead
that is a love impossible to trace back to any body
freely formed in the absence of trajectory despite
the incessant recursion of divide and thresh and divide
again in the familiar pattern of a pine tree as viewed
from above which is very far away into the future
which is also how time comes accidentally into being
not the lifespan we refuse ourselves but the iteration
of the everything making and remaking itself as though
somehow a system might ever become more than
a morning where someone is packing and someone else
waits in the bathroom happy for an eventual leaving
or the circuitous wind sweeps fallen leaves into an exiting
path or the standard method whereby chaos becomes
love circling back to augment a theory of being
we imagine first as stasis which is also how the body
becomes not-so-accidentally a meta-expression
our syntax again of want then want then want again

original being

my father holds my life above his head
as he would hold a cudgel or a pickax

he stands like this
with my life
in his hands for a very long time

the oceans fret him foam
his round head makes a wolf moon

he begs prophets to fight him
he gnashes the earth with his feet

he commits to a suspicion of angels
his heart
an artillery of attempts

he bends at his waist
flexes his arms
he swings at the earth with my life

god of joy

the choice afforded a body to live is the first
criteria for joy
to choose to live instead of dying

a poem can honeycomb a day in joy
but not kill the fear of being killed

i'm sorry
i've lingered too long at accident scenes
and seen too much

i need you to understand
i know myself to be a little crooked and off kilter

in a debate
you'd probably determine i'm no contest at all
you'd be wrong

you might say *she's a delinquent*
running around in the woods and i'd have no ethos
worth defending

i'm talking about the thrill of argument
which is the same as hunting
which i have a taste for

don't underestimate my warning
i will outlast you
i was a lurch called girlhood until the cancer came

but even before

after the beating
i'd already hardened

i'm within a few feet of that landslide vowel
that could make you love me if
oh
only i could be honest

i am six years old on the floor of an alley being
kicked in the head

i hear the n-word for the first time
so the word means the same thing as *kick*
the word means glass on pavement under me
means

two girls spitting
two girls punching
two girls leave me bleeding

be finished
lower your eyes
say   *you don't have to end badly*
i 'll forgive you

what's broken in me is vowel
shaped like a mouth
round enough to swallow
the world

theorem for a body

in the assemblage of my common life
the body perpetuates a racial algorithm
bending marigolds forward in early fall

the freeway goes where it will
cars are new again and again
the air clogged in newness

my backyard will cluster red
orange
fence a common avoidance of conversation
equate the distance to love deduced

(*let's do the math*): you are i are thou
exponentially

(*as in*) :
temperature determines
dew point
(*as if*) :
hope inhabits our sum
as monstrous as hope means to be

marigolds in fact are not necessarily
the original trajectory points of coming to be or
the result of how planes intersect inevitably

how i'll be made consecutive examples
of weary bliss riddled against one another

or the theory of a hot air balloon

creeping toward a sensible horizon
and the smitten mountains not so far

i perish the infinite promises
trumpet my blunt mortality

psalm

i exact a posture of faith
depart the great unruined

hold still this beating heart

i bow to gods and they bow back
i think of fleeing often

i cede my scarlet body-dream
i try again to harness sun

the fish are plenty but also sick
the leaves stoic
arrogant

pollen infers
an eventual coming

the waters have turned plastic
the toads are long since blind
doves litany relentless
bees pool instead of swarm

i exhaust divine indifference
i see blood sometimes in the street

hold still my beating heart

we may no longer consider the end

a time for birds dies sometime between
when robert kennedy jr
disappears and the berlin
wall comes down
hope is pro forma
we begin to talk about shelf life
our parents
think they're getting somewhere
i can't tell you
what to make of this now without
also saying
when i was 19 and read in a poem
the pure products of america go crazy
i felt betrayed
my father tells me not to whistle because
i am a girl
he gives me my first knife and says
keep it in my right hand and
keep my right hand in my right
pocket when i walk at night
he shows me the proper kind of fist
the sweet spot
on the jaw
to leverage my shorter height
upper cut someone down
there are probably birds on the long
walk home but
i don't remember them
because the pastoral
is not meant for
a young god

with a fist in each pocket
waiting for a reason

in regard to the soul

by the seventh year
there are too many
answers in the world

i stop sleeping

sometimes
a siren
sometimes
falling disquiet

i wonder where
how
it's june

i unwind my sheets
a humid fit
leave the nightmare of my last life:

a boy
a red shirt
a yellow field
bloomed
a courtyard

i leave my bed
hear no breathing in the night
my parents nowhere outside

i'm barefoot panic
check next door

lights-off
run two blocks another way
no one

i'm a small body in ruffled pajamas
a nylon psychedelic print
roaming
a dark expanse that inspires me
to renounce
gravity
unhinge myself
from the world again

stars hiss
morning yawns open
the worn-down mountains

i run past dumpster-rot
climb stairs where i'll break
my ankle in a month
enter our apartment
the hall
my parents' room

my asthmatic-heave
fills their doorway
finds them
sleep-heavy under
a strand of moon

my parents remain this way
for the rest of
this life

a silhouette outside of which
i'm entirely alone

the world at my back
blinking

in regard to monsters

a high trill ancestors
my sleep

squared blue notes
above the beneath

i'm awake
am i dreaming?

the sound isn't a milkman
bringing my gram cheese and butter

not my dad asleep in a town
that's forgotten its indigenous name

not his grandfather's father still
a union soldier in death

that old white man who haunts my study
asks for whiskey at night

his voice
creation-pitched

his soul unhitched by ether
bounding full speed

god of what's almost forgotten

we come from the same heaven
i love his rotten tooth

he wears
levi's with a worn pocket

i wear nothing
important to this story

i watch the world propagate
his monstrous manhood

he shakes when he raises a mug to his mouth
i never leave my body

when he finishes with me i pity him
forever failing

he knows
i am stronger

i know
knowing never ends

god of earth

you will hate me
unmake me

utter me
lilt

first
you'll touch me softly

last
uproot my calm

behold
your shored ascent

god of gods

i

your father is a truck
sumac in the first yard
he owns
thinks he owns
inexplicably forgetting
the work of owning
the body
so his body is also
only-ness

one june you wear
a white lace dress
he embraces you in a photo
which stirs fractals
into other chaos
some release
in your being-
ness
out here
outside *you*
made you-
ness

summer
your skin burns
the first time
ever
cheeks both
brown and pink

eyelids smarting
the lake beach
blurred
sailboats
fins
coasting the water

a man you barely know
says he could skin you
easily
hang the shape of your
carcass
on his wall

you carry your knife
more often

when he dies soon after
you're relieved
but finally know
the unexplainable
concept of *you*
your hands throbbing
bone and blood
your muscled reflection
your thinning
atmosphere

you count
twenty six years
earlier when
you write a poem to

your father who then
was one year
older
than you are
now

you regret
authoring time
this way
as distance between you
crouched and meaningful
though poems
you also lace
in time

ii

little one
harping my reaches
deaf to my call
forgive
what you devour

god of never again

in the beginning
my black body is gold
a storied summer

everything an old soul needs for a new
life on a small planet

then
i am raised like a poor white girl to have
no hope in the world

i ask sleep to remember what i am
i have something to do with fire
lightening

i have every need to be angry
i am easy-access-wrath

here's how i locate why rage feels easy:
the world populates a fury of accidents

a nudge
out of favor
may ignite me

whoever i am churns lava in her sleep
she can't remember herself
either

she remembers only
i am all flame

god of lost bodies

i'm a scarce wish
a half-done past

a tenuous rib
i am the arch

beneath your heart cramp
your deciduous reach

the splenetic
fabric of your spine

i am the night's
stampede

i am an ancient tree
named for a horse

who kills itself there
shhh

you are sugar
and breath

my lavish sin
my mauve undertaking

your last blood
your orange moon

i am forbidden

you are loveless

according to the lilies
my mouth is empty

hold me until
you are stone

ii

the last gods

we were joy junkies riding coal waste on old mining roads
the white birch divining subtle vibrations of earth
railroad tracks ribboning orange the sinking sun

what prone light enters un-feathered
what larva   what salt   what white can unmake
spine cloud tripe pity

she was in love with the guy who was in love
with her best friend   he was white-blonde long
she was white-freckled sweet

we lived to be night   but alive
no stars shined brighter than our bodies
outlined by fire

there were two white girls and one black girl walking
the neighborhood of another black girl   the neighborhood
girl tells the new black girl   walk in front   not in back

what enters unformed horizon breaks
not continuums   though you refuse
to imagine an end

a cloaking theory whitens sky when i
finally arrive at my inner
constitution

it takes me too long to learn that *pretty* is a white
myth that ends in death   death is a field

white with trees if we could see them

they are running with masks
they are running without masks
the street is bound in movement

the sirens become a direction
the light is white in the background
the light near white almost

the sheet is white over his face
a white shard seeds me
i have two knives instead of a heart

white boils down to rum when it begins as sugar
the ruins pock the island at the beginning
and end of our romance

white wears heels   looks
over her shoulder
white knows what she's done

i've been gone a long time
each day is a room
the landscape only water and hills

if you widen your focus we become a map
you can't distinguish your water from my water
your hills from my hills

when i refuse to love the island
the sea turtles come   they bury their eggs so deep
only a mongoose can find them

we were going to change the world
we couldn't press charges
he was obviously unarmed

she does not pull over
the dead boy is everything for everyone
everything means captive   after all

clarity is not white
i write this down and think i'm happy
wanting white to be a lie

it rains both inside and out   the world is genius
and smoke   i'm sitting here because of nothing
you did   please don't call me lovely

if you hunt
there is white beyond the canopy of leaves

if you're prey
there is red within the canopy of trees

regardless
there is light of some dark doing

a white boy calls a landscape my hip
he marbles me exotic
he watches the way
i write his name like mine

beyond something of shadows
a vase with roses holds the skull of a woman

loved by every hand that touched her

don't confuse a trumpet flower
for yellow sentiment
pollination is a thug fight

what heart thump legions these still stars
what molten revolt adorns the claw
what prone light enters un-feathered now

iii

how to battle

widen your stance
weaponize a slow slump of sheep grazing
father the grass beneath them
anger each prayer
defeat first your waning want
defeat next the coming mark
vein the horizon with your death undoing
live
refuse the placid moon
flock to fist
hammer your way out
or in
assume the empirical formula of ancestors
so they taste your breath
so they wince
true

the summer i am not murdered

i go to the woods to find my life
and my life changes
the road
loses me no matter which legend i follow
i've forgotten how to hear the stars
the pavilion mutes my angles against a fawn
wobbling in ferns   down this road   a woman
smears her face with every color she imagines
she ruins herself by loving love
the water says
you've wandered far too far from home
what i've never been able to say is true
begins with rust on the underside of a bridge
and a stream that smells from sulphur
and a scream that sounds like july
if i never felt his hands on my throat
i'd never have held a knife to his chest
but i did
i felt his blood-bloom
his chakra
his heart

in regard to being a woman

i learn to love a blade by deboning
a chicken with a perfect knife
it's not that a small heart
must be cut in a clean line
just that we understand the way
an object feels the difference
between the way we hold a knife and
the way we hold a lover
the way we hold a pen is nothing
like the way we hold a knife
an object doesn't have to be
sharp to save us
anything can become a grenade
though explosion is a thing of leaving
while sharpness is a thing of longing
i can hold a pen like a weapon
i can hold a key between two fingers
straight out like a spike
and call it *how to walk home*
i can use the tin tag of a hotel keychain
to slice open the eye of a guy following me
through the streets of portland
it would be so easy
subtle like a kiss i land
on his mouth mid-sentence
the blind-side of a sharp thing
the only thing he'll remember

my body a jagged line

for as much of this life as i remember
i prepare to survive the day
my mother dies

i wait for it
as you'd wait for something inevitable
but unscheduled
like a flood

i sign my name like hers
i manifest misgiving
i tend to her by phone

i reimagine my mother as bread
a measured precision
a series of steps

or as the world
subsiding

i call each day
say   *mother!*
she says
daughter!

we laugh like this as though
the day will never come

anthropos

my brother calls at 4 a.m.
late october
she's gone

the sky streaked that morning
heartlessly
the most exquisite tangerine-blue

as if to say my mother's death
meant nothing against
the terror nature makes of beauty

i fail to
renounce the metropolis
as a dead poet once said we should

the hunger of my small city
darkly manifests
my more enormous appetite for grief

the world
devours itself
regardless

the mountain forests spindle
oxygen
against our grit cities

the sated concrete avenues
seem safer
than returning to the woods

i regret the plastic bottles
i've used
the ways i've webbed our ruin

our extinction lyrics the earth's
full belly
its garment of bones

disambiguation

the free egg-stand on county line road
charges six dollars a dozen since the election

the barn is sold
the tire swing disappeared

the pond edged in cattails
explodes through late October

catches an angle of sun so tangerine
mountains pay forward pink shadow in gratitude

everything in sight costs something
to someone

on this part of my drive
i talk to my dead mother in my head

thank her
or apologize
plead with her absence

we talk about white fear
the terror of seeing your body erased

not mine
hers

not what i am but
what i was in my mother's white body

a helix assigned an inevitable blackness
growing inside
then born

iv

god of always

if my whole body were an eye
where is the hearing?

if my whole body were hearing
where is the smelling?

i am an utterance of many ruins
and you love me

a body to whom all things are known
a body of secret things
a body long-promised a long journey
a body incited

you are a whole engraved story day and night
i am a flood and you tell the story of flood

i am they who are born in the hills
you are they in their gorgeous robes

i give to you the love of a woman
you name a god *where love begins*

we hold each other like bulls
we lock our horns in embrace

we altar joy against dark
we jewel our breasts beautiful

long after nowhere
our bodies begin

in regard to marriage

in the end we never say goodbye
in the beginning we're a string of fractures
afterwards my body is again free
your mind never pieces together the torment
everything i ever say is a lie
i shoulder the last truth you have
he told me to be flattered to be chosen
she whispered the word mother like a curse
that night i dreamt i killed him before he killed me
our hearts aren't the real hosts of joy
northern lights came to pennsylvania that summer
we stood silently watching their abyss
we set out to manifest lives elsewhere
the desert never wanted us
the desert would never leave us
the woods weren't lovey-dovey either
loving everything means also loving nothing
we never wanted to be beautiful
i can't make a whole story of us
i don't remember laughing
we loved the dog equally
you never wanted to not want me
we'll always defer the carnage
i can't bring your words to life
the poem skips to our end
we saw a bear on the way to our vows
good and bad omens remain mostly the same
the tiny minister seemed in so much of a hurry
laurel branches snagged her purple robes
your mother hated me though we had the same name
she was a staunch advocate of hygiene

i understand how she ruined you
i anchor myself in shallow water
i anchor myself and still go adrift
i'm sorry to have not mentioned my volcano
you never marry again
i marry which is a mistake
a boundary i shouldn't have crossed
blood has only the past and the future begging

god of doorways

to love me means
i become a satin tide

i become a sunflower flute
a dim missive supplanting oil spills

as if the earth is responsible for its own duplicity
to be loved by me means you become a tempered mule

a pillow-dune
a brisk silence moleculed in ozone

when i fall out of love
i cleave abandoned quarries

i sigh beyond the coordinate system
my azimuth makes of a celestial pulse

i configure a lugubrious summit
a woeful slip of rapture dimmed

to un-love me means forgetting the scent
of lilac but not lilac's compound clusters

means living between the joy of a thing
and the thing itself

beginning with the debris of how
i end in magenta again

my volcano hushing pacific tide

my fleet-spill wailing gulls

my singular gravity
star-sliced

divination

a dead man tells me he has a twin
it's a she
he whispers
smiles
frowns down into the nothingness
heaven makes

he tells me he never wanted things to work out this way
i know
i know
nod
i can't touch him

he asks me to find this twin
gives me a word for safe keeping
a word for which i know no meaning

in a lost language
it could mean *clearness* but also mean *bloom*
it could mean
sprightliness of a look
(as of: a parched field after rain; as of: a hungry woman after a meal)

it could mean *the first fruits of the season* or *any novel thing* or *the prime of youth*
it might mean *a range of "no"*
as in *denying or dissenting*
as in *an eternal no-ing*

there is no living word for the word of the dead that means *wear a*
garment   with purpose
my language is no place or object

no ghost or girl he imagines his twin

today
she is dead   too
her death
isn't for the better or for the worse
her death means nothing in every language

the dead man knows
i needed to know
a word without meaning is free

V

the body seldom chooses

recent joys -- of which there are many
meaning there's quiet and snow covering everything

ice crackled footsteps outside a happiness
i can't clearly explain to my ancestors yes it's freezing

and people take their bodies outside so cold blued to bone
seems most for the fun of coming back inside to warm

and drink tea and laugh about how cold how cold the body says
in shivers and flushed skin seeking fire and other bodies

against which to huddle unless the fire becomes untame and seers
a field elsewhere outside swallows high grass in hiss-snap

electrical lines flailing a wind that feeds the fire a row of houses
wrapped in christmas lights in wind that howls toward the east

wind that takes the fire with it feeds the fire a whole neighborhood
then another even though snow will cover everything

tomorrow which brings me back to recent joys
like having hot coffee delivered right to my door this morning

or my dogs who blame me for nothing or my daughter who
i'm speaking to again after five years of not allowing her

inside my home where i am safe now though that joy is salty
and short-lived since it's so hard to forget loving her there

in a way that's easy and determined like the story of my body not
having a child and her body born from another woman's body

which she'll punish me for always even though i'm proud
sometimes like the night she drives through the burned away

ice encrusted neighborhood loading singed dogs and cats
into her old Honda clenching each time she hoists a whimpering

body onto the seat as though she had not ever betrayed me or taken
everything i had and left me penniless in the middle of another winter

years ago when the inside of my home was not burning away
with the driving firestorm that leveled the neighborhood due south

but just collapsed on top of us as love failed to cure anything
after we expected it would cure everything unlike the sharp eyes

of a horse let loose from its corral as the fire spread and safety
would be something the horse needed to find for himself

which he does not know as flames send him running madly
in every direction because the horse knows only that flames move

flames can be everywhere and this story his body tells in full
gallop captured in a photo by a passing stranger who fragments

the horse the trees the flames as terror stilled which i want
to call beautiful but don't when my daughter sends me the image

i don't tell her that her weeping body knows the awful
canter of joy fleeing before the snow and the ruins.

vi

inception

in the morning's aural unbuttoning
first something warbles at the edge of a biting chill

then something of pink crawls along the near-ridge
backs up to a retreating after-midnight-blue

still familiar
like the opening scene in a movie i've seen
where a famous director filters light to some

transmittance of calm so that i now easily impose my memory
of that staged morning onto this scene of actual morning

and consider which is more or less a disappointment while i sip
cold coffee
look out the west window past bird to the idea

of bird
see it as movement and sound
no smell
no teeming lice under-wing
no decaying chick
splayed at the base of that tree

i settle this deference
the red tail swooping into updraft
instead of rabbit-flesh

a glass-glint movement against water
a made world tethered in doing

psalm

i remember the grouse but not the sound
the grouse makes
is it a hornet buzz or a chortle

tenor suffocating the laurel
or a lithe note of air
barely audible

i remember the pith of my voice but
nothing i ever said
my tongue wed to the dank season

a repose
perhaps
an unlucky tremor

what singed prayer
shimmers my name   what pooled
charge becomes my lash

what fickle release has me undone imagine
i am a bullet cast among the tulips
a brash course
within a blur of tenderness

what is my subject
does my name matter to the dead

i swim the creek softly
scrape the moss as though it's politic
spiral the predictable shimmer of water
mistaken for light

the innocent

    at the center of my life
a woman tells me of a dead whale
she's discovered on the beach
its flotsam flesh peeling
toward sand
    feasting gulls bridge
the way between death
and surviving death
unbind blubber and bone
dislodge an eye brined by foam
    the whale's soul travels
easily in space
rivers a path among stars
heedless sundered in silence
thicker than ocean
    death sees the body first
from very far away like an old
friend she'd meet on the beach
who she'd watch poke a whale's eye
with a stick
    the whale travels slowly to her next life
feels the stick pierce a bodily memory
bobbing in the tide of that life
a swollen stank-obligation
wafting heavily on the breeze

our agreeable end

i watch hours of
network news

deduce that we're
almost out of time

our buoyant humanity
useless after all

we watch the next tsunami
digitize our disasters

i don't know how to deny
the end

i look up a word
i can't pronounce

irrefragable
not to be contested

i can no longer dispute
the beginning

i can't imagine myself
beyond

being able to
beyond trying

thinking about the best
place

the newest report
how we spin our joy

cloak our shoulders
in laughter

the powers that be
disclose what's possible

people going about
a secret rising

i've been a witness
since the day i was born

someone blasts bass beats
in the street

the gulf coast
the gulf coast rising

think about water and
there it is again

the inventory of decline
the newest something

different
and so the same

order of being

i mean never again
to speak of god-silence

to grieve their habitat
or fear forgetting

they inhabit the rain and
the space within rain

inhabit the magnolia that lined
my street in st louis

the moment i turned from the chalky
brown buff of their under-leaf

i mean to leave and fail

the gods know how much
i think of them

little eyelids tersed
little brain unleashed

i mean never again to willow
a day in pleading

to summon will and want
until will and want replace my gods

i un-sermon their psalms
until my sky is free

god of worship

i give you forest
you walk the sharp edge
of a lichened cliff
looking down
as though no one has ever
given you anything

i give you the tin sound of
your own heart
beating irregularly
on the side of the road

you listen to its rust-webbed
circumference
as though hearing
death speak for the first
time

i give you the teal depth of each
year up until now
paper the walls with each day
trim the sills
until the house is full

you shoulder a chill
remember the door
left open

i give you my voice
you reach forward
grab air

i give you the book of my summers
you give me another
version of me
a dulcet aftertaste
against

in regard to beginning

      years later
i forgive you
the summer's
pitch makes all things
impossible possible

      you are a milky
circumstance under a buck moon
i am reckoning without worry

      i cast myself against the flick
mouth of a shallow river
you wade against the moonlight
as though you're alone

      you never turn to see me
i swallow
the moon as though i am
light birthing a body

      in the dark current
our nakedness doesn't matter
we're not banished

      in the life that follows
we unbind ourselves
from the variable echo of
beginning

      we refuse omens from birds
either in flight

or at rest
close our many eyes
unsee the overpass

     under which we park the car
exit
walk in different directions
we take our curses elsewhere

     we quiver
the indifference of knowing
the world has always
intended to leave us

in regard to eclipse

the window doesn't open
so i can't hear the raw
rattle of bunchgrass straddling
the basin beneath
foothills i've come to love
because i've forgotten
the inwardness of sky
like you might forget the hands
of a person who saved you

by *you* i mean the last broken
version of me still a wary girl
mottled with rage
walking the night as though
she were the hunter and not
the hunted

by what velocity
do i measure the tremor
her wings make as a far-galaxy
collapses within her

how do i tell her the marrow
of her future is made

she lives
finds herself in this now
supine on the couch against
a hush view of cowbirds
dizzy in bullrush
their calls

sigil the air in shrill reason

by *survive* i mean
she's here
still knuckles each day
like a threat

god of every day since

consider the saddest day
in the history of what's true about our country

we will always want to be saved
by the next election

even the deer
conspire to seek truth

hapless at roads
dead everywhere

prone to compulsive
darting into collision

the road is an invitation
not the kind

where you wake up
with a view of the ocean

how did it happen
someone will ask

in our guts we know
these narratives of misfortune

each night
i rehearse:
if an enemy anticipates
my defense   i'll never   be free

we had a game like this in college
it took weeks to finish

no one ever won
which is why we called it *risk*

we are so happy
to have stolen these places

we are so happy
to have regrown the woods

we're americans in love
with ourselves

and our brutal
becoming

godling

you know me by now
i don't believe in someday anymore
they have all the power
anything they want
silence
sirens

i'm watching a movie where everyone has the same black
rectangular phone and so every call becomes the same

we don't suspect one another
i listen to your voice very carefully
you listen to mine
my breathing

i imagine you with your last lover
your chests bare
wet
while you talk in the morning
shower
steam
towels on the floor
i want to be jealous but don't understand

i've done what i've done through the brown loops of warblers
that make no boundaries or neighborhoods
i know them as bliss

i mean to say
a black body feels
any moment

our full hands
our hearts
our best things
turn to air

gods of measure

someone has forgotten again to see
a boy instead of a target

these days   there are always
photos and video and sometimes sound

if the image goes viral   we can't help
but make poems

in another world a woman is walking
too heavily on the old wooden stairs of a building

two-quarter-time just as i hear outside
a skateboard accent cement in rolling breaks

she slams the microwave
i think   *she is a territorial thing*

i knew girls like her   a middle daughter
stomping around a house

her mother yelling
no stomping

when her mother dies her father
is busy running everything

the daughter
stomps like that forever

slams the cupboard
the window   the door

fills every hallway so someone will know
she's present in the world

she's an anchor of sound
familiar

we could be grown women who talked
about brothers who were killed

instead of our mothers
who died
but then
how

i only ever wanted to survive
being a child

our dialect of injury makes us
mean maybe more to one another

maybe we mean less
when we pretend there's no soul

if we've learned anything at all
we've learned shelter

the young poets   how they still
love to make things beautiful

even the one and only-ness

they feel

they still remember the body's
viral expansion of light

the heavy sound on the stairs
is no matter in the scheme of this poem

which is why a girl   feeling un-present
or a boy   who becomes a target

could never love a poet
especially a young one

incapable of loving anyone
more than a mute-bright star

god of wanting to know where to be

today a politician told a press conference
the world is a gangster and because it seemed apparent

that he found poetry in the savagery of his job
i felt happier when i walked away from the broadcast

the hope i held onto made me feel new
in the way it dismissed everything i've learned to be true

it's sunday and i'm not calling my father yet to interrupt
his day of waiting without my mother again   or

to intercede with the reminder my voice brings
she is the greatest thing we have in common

and the greatest thing we no longer have between us
on sundays   someone goes to home depot

gets lumber   brings it home   all one needs to do is take it
out back   someone else may come   give next steps   it will be

only so long before somebody decides it was a good job
or a bad job   it's always something   the outcome

my sister's not working this summer   the school busses
driven across valley roads are driven without her driving them

not working is a thing she says every day in a way that makes it
so directly related to working that they are in some ways essentially

the very same thing   working and not working   driving and not driving
my sister is a poor white loop of active negation in the face of being

i cannot remember why i was upset with annie lamott and gave
all her books away   i remember feeling that when she repeated

profoundly
the words of a dying friend

i would remember   them forever
though i've forgotten

but also
a certain thievery was at hand

i've learned   all words   are forgiveness   as in
to forgive someone for something you cannot remember

is more simple   like just loving someone enough
i post an article about whales and sea turtles

caught in fishing nets off the west coast
their abandoned protections

mean there will be no caps enforced
no fisheries shut down

no sanctions
no dissuasions and so the whales and the sea turtles

suffer the sum   consequence
flat ontology of kelp

i imagine within new ontologies   equitable objects
become   the trampled currency of value —

valued objects and unvalued
objects

the reassignment of the turtle
as a value-object

i imagine can only happen via
the sound of sobbing coming

from every window in the world
at once

on the fourth of july   a white woman
called the police on a black man wearing socks in the pool

two weeks after a white woman called
the cops on a black girl selling water

a month after a white woman called
the cops on a family in a park 2 weeks after

a white woman called the cops on a college
student in her own dorm sometime around the same

time as a black woman called the cops on a man
who would not let her enter her own gated community

where she lived as a doctor and
he didn't live at all

then   in a determined turn of circumstances
someone dies again

flashing lights
flicker in the path of the soul as it rises

finally   a crescendo
then the world collapses

here's where a smooth poet would say something funny
and demeaning about her height or weight or self-esteem

or her relationship with her mother   or sex
and perhaps there might be a moment also where she describes

her own reflection in a way that makes you laugh
at her awkward   but snapdragon posture

when i was 20   i sat on a lawn in green bay
and cried because i could not save the world that night

i fell short of my fundraising quota
4 hours door to doubtful door

collecting $12 checks to clean up
toxic waste

i could not tell the difference between
having cancer and being black but either way

a clipboard said something about something
i still looked forward to a world at peace

some hate hadn't yet begun   there are so
many worlds we'd rather not have been part of

which is a privilege of being   to say *what not* after the fact
i knew nothing about the station at othello park except

a beautiful poet posted a photo which should have been
all about lines but seemed all about curves   space   and light

i felt moved to a longing that made me feel
at once an orphan but also someone who abandoned the world

the photo gave my feeling a look
gave it a roof   a large window   hint of shadow

light   in this image   had no consequence
except as a vehicle of exposure

in another universe
 i was born and lived and died

the beautiful poet's photo in this life
reconciles

the absence of myself despite myself
with myself

without anyone further
the same

god of what comes next

life begins
as a river
a preamble to
sky's bluest
footprint
a willowy brink
or a bracket of
flowers

i am no marksman
anyway
no horizon pitch
though the edge
of creation
pleads my pose

please

and i go on
abate the blade
death makes of
leaf
hornet
a cavity of ribs
once flesh drops
away

i make the body
fault
liable
a profit lost

eventually
please
i hear most often

i peril
the luck of genius
ambling
a synapse storm
temper of cells

you begin
as flail beneath
grief
circling
a mad pool
ache
pushed from stars
my pulse

exegesis

you'll meet a guy in a red hat checking his phone with the gait of someone fallen
in our wild center
they won't kill him because he is just some guy on his phone which means he's
whiteness on his phone
which means walk here and here and there
it's good
go ahead
you're safe
still
he's someone who values the new economy
it's easy like this
a currency of berries means something like blood but not blood
something taken in and turned body-black
money has nothing to do with ducks but everything to do with how we use them

here's what happens:
somewhere deep within any state there is a man who would kill me
first
he'd kill my safe distance
next
he'd kill my other-where-ness so that only here means only him and my death
waiting
he'd kill
my yet-to-come

kill the way my words meant more than his words and then again
thereafter sticky skin and knives and all my teeth scattered there
because my face is a ballot and his knife is the campaign against me

i as we say
am not part of this transaction

here are my directions:
be messy and loud
use profanity like sugar
think of killing like you think of napalm
as a thing of the past and the present we call now
the problem isn't coming to know
they crave the other as a specific hunger
they barter the reeds
what does this mean in human language is not
so much a question as a defense

in the midst
midst can be ever-present

we frame the --ism
he's just another man which means he is just another man who may kill me or
may not kill me and so seems lost within the privilege and the act

someone has said
how much is she worth? can we buy her? how much will she fetch? will you buy her?
the market dropped

we are as worthless as we imagine after so many years of appreciation and flags
the pond makes revolution wane

the reeds still the love of gunshot
adorn our petitions

you'll have questions
*what is the narrative of lost trajectories? when do we learn our pockets are empty? how is
a debit card declined?*
your wants are everything and nothing

god   here
could save me

they paid me with a bridge and a creek and a burden called
here body   here body   here body   let's see you

the protesters will shout go away

go away america

go back to your bloody start

go to your horse

your field

your chains

the patriarchy is made of flagstone and bricks

politics begin with wheat

what waste do you enjoy which i mean not so much as a question but as an
assault

you are caged within this wind regardless

here's my narrative:
the wild innerness has no honor which means
it kills more than it can eat

that guy
the one with no home
he stands on a bridge and looks at the koi
he looks at himself less often

in seeing he thinks *direction* thinks *bewildered*
his end is not obvious but made
eventually
the pond yields a stink unwarranted
i mean a manifesto of sleeping
the market smells of sex and paper money
sour dirt
my arm costs less than my legs

what he steals from me
what he steals from me makes the debt between us
shudder

here's what i owe:
i un-product the plains
i un-slaughter the us of me and them
i am who they are and who i am

i'm surprised at the night's depravity
remember the honest want of more than enough of what i need to need but have
forgotten
no
what i need to need and remember then forget every morning   i have   we have
yes
he is an idiot who will kill me in such a delicate way his generals think it art
the slice from my chin to my gut so clean it barely bleeds

understand we are
each of us
a job
he will own you this way
he is how murder begins and should you want to know more you should know
murder begins with desire which is the only free thing
beauty is cheap
the massacres
a resource
an autopsy that ends in the black

here's what you do when the country you live in soils itself:
go to the pond and write an epistle of how things should begin or how they
should end or how the ending and the beginning are their own cartel

here's what i do:
smuggle canadians over the border
keep track of the overhead
is my loan under water
are my lungs in foreclosure
carpet bomb the last silos of nebraska and call it solving patriarchy
i mean an epistle of the flaccid
of glory be
survive the profit margin up
and vocabulary
in chaos i find a way to smooth it over
to make another without the chilly theft of reason which doesn't exist in the
wood or in the alleys of hoboken

blue and red are both consigned to overdraft
the distal end of the body so emptiness is nowhere to go back to
i mean an epistle of where to be

look at him

his expensive wrench

dismantle yourself

my hands cost more than my feet

my jaw is free with my skull

lacquer my ribs which are two for one and assemble a chandelier as antlers are

assembled likewise

my body is contraband

my way is inflated

my will is a recession waiting to happen

my absence of

out there is a trap

if i kill him first

i'll be what i'm supposed to be

here are my directions:
make sure the knife is clean and sharp
put five dollars between my teeth
walk through the center of town with my arm in the air
with the knife in my hand
with money in my mouth

if i have not yet been shot and killed say i will not be
i will not be inventoried
say i will not be sold
where there is decadence there is no art because there is no discussion of what rot
we make   i cannot write myself out of my story
my body is all i have

when i cash out at the end of the night my profits say
i can kill a man easily with no remorse
i have always known this and can't say so
i will do it for free
i mean an epistle of teeth scattered as he would scatter mine
no one will notice that done is done and done means the same as undone

here are more instructions:
tell everyone the revolution is silent
so listening is useless
say "no" most often
say empty
say
now it's time to go
the sky will fall as we say it will
buy low and sell high
murder don't murder how easily it is to do so
don't easily do
i mean an epistle of unsaying
don't so easily be what i'm supposed to be
there are two worlds
before and after
i am gutted and so in turn undo
unready
go out in the world
out in the world i go and i
the gutted
gut

viii

last life

i end with so much to forget
the assassinations
the protesters

the migrant workers picking tomatoes
barefoot in the field of a corporate farm

aerial images of recurring pyramids
a man's bones
holding his husband's bones after a volcano
ashes them to ether

in summer i met the names of orchids
pittsburgh's yellow bridges
an amish boy running toward a barn
red gardenias
an elk-king crossing the road in traffic
a journalist
beheaded
his wife
a character in the movie
the fringe date palm of shadow
in desert sun
the milky persistence of birth
zodiac vectors claiming sky
the disappearance of woods
again

acknowledgements

I cannot express enough gratitude and affection for all of the souls at Omnidawn Press, especially Rusty Morrison and Laura Joakimson, for welcoming me into the family-spirit of their vocation with devotion and love. Many thanks to the National Endowment for the Arts, MacDowell, the Vermont Studio Center, the Cave Canem Foundation, the Poetry Foundation, the Center for African and African American Poetry at the University of Pittsburgh, and those publications in which some of these poems, in some form, appear -- *Poetry Magazine, Best American Poetry, the Indiana Review, Poem-a-Day, Entropy, Interim, The Kenyon Review.* Thank you, Ronaldo Wilson, Ross Gay, Adrian Matejka, Tyehimba Jess, Major Jackson, Jen Benka, Mary Gannon, Dawn Lundy Martin, Nicole Dutton, Arline Dowling, Jacquie Scott, Tyrone Williams, Sue Zemka, Nan Goodman, Susan Briante, Sheriffa Gallaway, and Eldridge Greer for your energy and support. I offer appreciation and thanks to Jim Schley, Vanessa Angélica Villarreal, Prageeta Sharma, Khadijah Queen, Jennifer Maddix, David Lehman, Carmen Gimenez Smith, and Monroe Rodriguez, who've each, in their own way, brought me to this writerly moment. I want to express my deepest unending gratitude, love, and affection to the women, to my poetry doulas, the coven, the matrices -- Michele Kotler, Marion Wrenn, Brenda Cardenas, Iris Dunkle, Robin Reagler, Nicole Callahan, Laura Cronk, Jane Creighton, Janet Jennerjohn, Catherine Prescott, Suzanne Wise, Bethany Price, and Kristin Peterson Kaszubowski. And to all of my dead -- thank you, each, for coming.

Ruth Ellen Kocher is the author of seven other books, *Third Voice* (Tupelo Press, 2016), *Ending in Planes* (Noemi Press, 2014), *Goodbye Lyric: The Gigans and Lovely Gun* (Sheep Meadow Press, 2014), *domina Un/blued* (Tupelo Press, 2013), Dorset Prize winner and the 2014 PEN/ Open Book Award, *One Girl Babylon* (New Issues Press, 2003) Green Rose Prize winner, *When the Moon Knows You're Wandering* (New Issues Press, 2002), and *Desdemona's Fire* (Lotus Press 1999) Naomi Long Madgett Prize winner. My poems and essays appear in *Letters to the Future: Black WOMEN/ Radical Writing, Renga for Obama, Angles of Ascent: A Norton Anthology of Contemporary African American Poets, Best Experimental Poetry, Black Nature, From the Fishouse: An Anthology of Poems that Sing, Rhyme, Resound, Syncopate, Alliterate, and Just Plain Sound Great, An Anthology for Creative Writers: The Garden of Forking Paths, IOU: New Writing On Money, New Bones: Contemporary Black Writing in America.* I have been awarded fellowships from the National Endowment for the Arts, the Cave Canem Foundation, MacDowell, and Yaddo. I am a Contributing Editor at *Poets & Writers Magazine* and Professor of English at the University of Colorado where I teach Poetry, Poetics, and Literature and currently serve as the Divisional Dean for the Arts and Humanities in the College of Arts and Sciences.

godhouse
by Ruth Ellen Kocher

Cover art byMichael Tella
cover art title: Queen of Ivory

Cover design by Laura Joakimson and Ruth Ellen Kocher
Interior design by Laura Joakimson
Cover typeface: Brother 1816
Interior typeface: Hightower and Brother 1816

Printed in the United States
by Books International, Dulles, Virginia

Publication of this book was made possible in part by gifts from
Katherine & John Gravendyk in honor of Hillary Gravendyk,
Francesca Bell, Mary Mackey, and The New Place Fund

Omnidawn Publishing
Oakland, California
Staff and Volunteers, Spring and Fall 2023
Rusty Morrison, senior editor & co-publisher
Laura Joakimson, executive director & co-publisher
Rob Hendricks, poetry & fiction editor, & post-pub marketing
Jason Bayani, poetry editor
Anthony Cody, poetry editor
Liza Flum, poetry editor
Kimberly Reyes, poetry editor
Sharon Zetter, poetry editor & bookdesigner
Jeffrey Kingman, copy editor
Jennifer Metsker, marketing assistant
Sophia Carr, marketing assistant
Katie Tomzynski, marketing assistant